1 MONTH OF
FREE
READING

at
www.ForgottenBooks.com

By purchasing this book you are eligible for one month membership to ForgottenBooks.com, giving you unlimited access to our entire collection of over 1,000,000 titles via our web site and mobile apps.

To claim your free month visit: www.forgottenbooks.com/free1297245

ISBN 978-0-428-96397-2
PIBN 11297245

For support please visit www.forgottenbooks.com

Cooperative
ECONOMIC INSECT
REPORT

Issued by

PLANT PEST CONTROL DIVISION

AGRICULTURAL RESEARCH SERVICE

UNITED STATES DEPARTMENT OF AGRICULTURE

Coo

AGRICULTURAL RESEARCH SERVICE

PLANT PEST CONTROL DIVISION

SURVEY AND DETECTION OPERATIONS

The Cooperative Economic Insect Report is issued weekly as a service to American Agriculture. Its contents are compiled from information supplied by cooperating State, Federal, and industrial entomologists and other agricultural workers. In releasing this material the Division serves as a clearing house and does not assume responsibility for accuracy of the material.

Reports and inquiries pertaining to this release should be mailed to:

Survey and Detection Operations
Plant Pest Control Division
Agricultural Research Service
United States Department of Agriculture
Washington 25, D. C.

Volume 11   May 5, 1961   Number 18

COOPERATIVE ECONOMIC INSECT REPORT

Highlights of Insect Conditions

GREENBUG infestations declining in most areas of Oklahoma and Texas; causing some damage to wheat in Curry, Quay and Roosevelt Counties, New Mexico; gradually moving north in Colorado. High populations can be expected in latter State with continued cool, dry weather. ENGLISH GRAIN APHID continues common in small grain in most areas of Oklahoma. CHINCH BUG infestations range heavy to light in south central and central Texas; spots being killed in some fields of young corn and milo in south central area. (p. 347). BROWN WHEAT MITE damaging dryland wheat in Texas and causing concern in southwest Kansas. ARMY CUTWORM damaging winter wheat in Williams County, North Dakota, and attacking same crop in southwest and south central South Dakota. (p. 348). ALFALFA WEEVIL adult activity increased on untreated alfalfa throughout Delaware; adults and larvae increasing on Eastern Shore of Maryland; infestations range light to severe in some areas of Virginia; damage heavy to fields in Oconee County, South Carolina, not treated during fall of 1960. (p. 349). PEA APHID continues heavy in Arizona; seriously damaging alfalfa in Virden Valley and is heavy in other areas of New Mexico; heavy on several crops in areas of Texas; moderate to heavy on alfalfa in most areas of Oklahoma; populations increasing in Delaware and New Jersey. SPOTTED ALFALFA APHID remains moderate to heavy in southwest Oklahoma. (p. 350).

PEACH TWIG BORER severe on peaches in Washington County, and active in Weber County, Utah. First PLUM CURCULIO adult jarred from peaches in Vincennes area and increasing at Carbondale, Indiana; half-grown larvae present in peaches at Reynolds, Georgia. (p. 352).

A WIREWORM (Conoderus lividus) damaging approximately 500 acres of tobacco in Gadsden County, Florida. (P. 355).

FACE FLY becoming active in several states. SCREW-WORM generally widespread over south and south central areas of Texas. (p. 359).

INSECT DETECTION: A PHYCITID (Euzophera ostricolorella) reported for the first time from Indiana. (p. 357). MEXICAN FRUIT FLY larvae found for first time in Starr County, Texas. WALNUT HUSK FLY collected for first time in Cache and Tooele Counties, Utah, during 1960 season. (p. 353).

CORRECTION   (p. 361).

SURVEY METHODS for Survey Entomologists. A presentation of the Committee on Insect Surveys and Losses of the North Central Branch, Entomological Society of America. (p. 363).

****

Reports in this issue are for week ending April 28, unless otherwise indicated.

WEATHER BUREAU 30-DAY OUTLOOK

MAY 1961

The Weather Bureau's 30-day outlook for May calls for temperatures to average below-seasonal normals over the northern half of the Nation and in the South Atlantic States. Above-normal temperatures are predicted for the Southwest and West Gulf States. In unspecified areas, near-normal temperatures are indicated. Precipitation is expected to exceed normal over the eastern third of the country and also the Pacific Northwest. Subnormal amounts are in prospect for the southwest quarter of the Nation, with near normal in unspecified areas.

Weather forecast given here is based on the official 30-day "Resume and Outlook", published twice a month by the Weather Bureau. You can subscribe through Superintendent of Documents, Washington 25, D. C. Price $4.80 a year, $2.40 a half year.

WEATHER OF THE WEEK ENDING MAY 1

Temperatures rose from much below-normal levels at the beginning of the week to well above by the end in the Far West, while the reverse was true in the East. The entire week was abnormally cold in the northern Great Plains, and seasonably warm in southern portions. Weekly averages were 9° to 12° below normal between the Great Lakes and Continental Divide. A low of 17° at Huron, South Dakota, on May 1 was the lowest ever recorded there in May during 81 years of record. In the Far West, freezing caused some crop damage in scattered areas. In the East, frost was reported as far south as North Carolina at the end of the week, but highs in the 80's occurred as far north as Pennsylvania at the beginning.

Frontal precipitation occurred almost daily in some northern areas and on 2 days in the lower Mississippi Valley and Southeast, but virtually none fell in southern Florida and from west Texas to the Pacific coast. Totals generally exceeded 1/2 inch east of lines joining Wichita, Kansas, with Milwaukee, Wisconsin, and Del Rio, Texas, except in Florida. Locally heavy rains occurred in the Midwest, and flooding continued in the Wabash River Basin in Indiana. Snowfall was reported as far south as northern Kansas, with falls ranging up to 2 inches at Stapleton, Nebraska, and northern portions of the Great Lakes region. In the Northeast, up to 4 inches of snow fell in mountainous areas, with a 5- to 10-inch cover now in northern Maine.

In the Far West, heavy rain and snow fell in the Cascades and Sierras of California, but elsewhere amounts were light. In Montana, light precipitation, following moderate to heavy amounts of the previous week, further alleviated the drought situation. Topsoil is now adequate in most sections of that State, although subsoil moisture continues deficient.

Numerous hailstorms and tornadoes occurred along with the rains in the Midwest and South. On the 30th, several tornadoes and unusually large-sized hail were reported in Oklahoma. On the 25th, tornadoes caused at least 8 injuries and destroyed several buildings in east-central Indiana.

Temperatures for April averaged from 2° to 6° below normal everywhere, except the extreme Southwest. For April 1960, temperatures averaged 2° to 6° above normal, except normal or slightly below in the Great Basin and Pacific Northwest. Precipitation for April 1961 is about the same as for April 1960. (Summary supplied by U. S. Weather Bureau).

CEREAL AND FORAGE INSECTS

GREENBUG (Toxoptera graminum) - KANSAS - Counts variable in wheat in southwest; range from less than 10 to 50 per linear foot of row. Populations estimated to be several hundred per linear foot in counties south of Finney County. Winged and wingless forms present. (DePew). MISSOURI - Light on oats, wheat and barley in central and north central areas; 0-4 per foot of row. (Munson, Thomas, Wood). OKLAHOMA - Populations in fields of grain declining in most areas. (Okla. Coop. Sur.). ARKANSAS - None found in northwest section of State. (Ark. Ins. Sur.). TEXAS - Severity of infestations slowly decreasing in most areas; considerable amount of control has been applied in Panhandle and Red River areas; however, light to moderate infestations still present. Grain in many fields beginning to boot and small percentage is in full head. Lack of moisture has slowed rapid growth in many areas of State. (Texas Coop. Rpt.). NEW MEXICO - Light to moderate, spotted infestations causing minor damage to wheat in Curry and Quay Counties; damaging wheat foliage in fields near Portales, Roosevelt County. (N. M. Coop. Rpt.). COLORADO - Gradually moving north in State. Winged forms averaged 2 per 100 sweeps in cereal crops in Adams County; present on barley in Morgan County; none found in northern portions of Larimer and Weld Counties. High populations can be expected with continued cool, dry weather. (Gausman, Jenkins).

ENGLISH GRAIN APHID (Macrosiphum granarium) - OKLAHOMA - Continued common in small grain in most areas of State. Most common species of aphid in small grain in northeast area, where counts ranged 25-125 per linear foot of row in fields checked. (Okla. Coop. Sur.). ARKANSAS - Light and decreasing in northwest area. (Ark. Ins. Sur.). MISSOURI - Light on wheat and barley in southeast area. (Munson, Thomas, Wood). ILLINOIS - Aphid counts in wheat, mostly this species, averaged 3 per sweep in west-southwest, 40 per sweep in southwest and less than one per sweep in east-southeast. (Ill. Ins. Rpt.). WISCONSIN - Averaged 2 per 50 sweeps, mostly alates, in grain in Iowa and Lafayette Counties; and one per 50 sweeps in Rock County; none found in Dane County fields. (Wis. Coop. Sur.).

APPLE GRAIN APHID (Rhopalosiphum fitchii) - OKLAHOMA - Although infestations continued common in small grain, populations reported to be on decline in most areas of State. (Okla. Coop. Sur.).

CORN LEAF APHID (Rhopalosiphum maidis) - ARIZONA - Infestations declined rapidly in barley statewide, due mostly to heavy parasitic and predatory action. Medium populations present in young sorghum and corn in central area. (Ariz. Coop. Sur.). NEW MEXICO - Light, spotty infestations in barley in Dona Ana, Chaves, Eddy and Luna Counties and in Virden Valley in Hidalgo County. (N. M. Coop. Rpt.).

WESTERN WHEAT APHID (Brachycolus tritici) - NEW MEXICO - Light to moderate, spotted infestations causing minor damage to wheat in Curry and Quay Counties. (N. M. Coop. Rpt.).

CHINCH BUG (Blissus leucopterus) - TEXAS - Infestations on young corn and grain sorghum range from heavy and widespread in south central area to light and local in central area. Spots being killed in some fields of young corn and milo in south central area. All nymphal stages and adults present in all fields, feeding on roots primarily. Control is very difficult. (Massey, McClung, Criswell, Newton). ARKANSAS - Only an occasional specimen taken in small grain in northwest area. (Ark. Ins. Sur.).

CORN FLEA BEETLE (Chaetocnema pulicaria) - ILLINOIS - Counts per 100 sweeps in wheat averaged 30 in west-southwest, 90 in east-southeast and 24 in southwest districts. Counts in grass in southwest district averaged 100 per 100 sweeps. (Ill. Ins. Rpt.).

HESSIAN FLY (Phytophaga destructor) - ILLINOIS - Averaged 3 per 100 sweeps in wheat in southwest district. In west-southwest, examination of puparia showed 67 percent of adults had emerged; eggs were also observed in this district. (Ill. Ins. Rpt.).

WINTER GRAIN MITE (Penthaleus major) - TEXAS - Infestations continue in many
fields in northern half of State, but further serious damage to small grains
unlikely. (Texas Coop. Rpt.).

BROWN WHEAT MITE (Petrobia latens) - TEXAS - Infestations light to heavy in
portions of upper Panhandle area, with considerable damage to dryland wheat;
controls underway on some irrigated wheat. (Gossett). KANSAS - Continues to
cause concern among wheat growers in certain areas of southwest; populations
decreased somewhat from previous counts but still average several hundred per
linear foot of row in heavily infested fields. (Depew). COLORADO - Averaged
2-5 per linear foot of row in cereal crops in Adams County; none found in Weld
and Larimer Counties. (Jenkins). UTAH - Present in dryland wheat at Promontory,
Box Elder County. (Knowlton). NEVADA - Light and spotted in alfalfa in Reno-
Sparks area, Washoe County. (Bechtel).

BANKS GRASS MITE (Oligonychus pratensis) - UTAH - Wheat in Logan area, Cache
County, heavily infested for so early in the season. (Davis).

EUROPEAN CORN BORER (Pyrausta nubilalis) - KANSAS - Overwintering mortality
averaged 91 percent in Jefferson County, which is much higher than usual.
(Burkhardt). NORTH CAROLINA - Adults began emerging April 18 at Aurora,
Beaufort County, and April 22 at Elizabeth City, Pasquotank County. (Lowry,
Chestnut, Farrier). DELAWARE - Pupation of overwintering larvae 26 percent in
New Castle and Kent Counties, 68 percent in Sussex County. (Burbutis, Mason).

CORN EARWORM (Heliothis zea) - FLORIDA - Early instar larvae serious on treated
corn in Bradenton area, Manatee County; 85 percent of ears infested in one
sample. Have apparently just appeared. (Kelsheimer). ARKANSAS - Activity
increased. Adults collected in light traps in northern and southern portions
of State. Egg deposition increasing on crimson clover in Faulkner County. (Ark.
Ins.Sur.).

ARMY CUTWORM (Chorizagrotis auxiliaris) - NORTH DAKOTA - Heavy and damaging 400
acres of winter wheat in Hardscrabble Township, Williams County; averaged 9 per
square foot along roadsides and 4 per square foot in winter wheat. Infestation
confined to area where hail and heavy rain occurred August 16, 1960. Experimenta
plots in infested area treated on April 21. (Post, Bradvick). SOUTH DAKOTA -
Attacking winter wheat in southwest and south central areas; populations low,
0-2 per 6 linear feet of row. (Mast). Damaging alfalfa in Perkins County.
(Hantsbarger). NEBRASKA - Some larval damage to wheat noted in Clay County;
however, plant growth appeared to be advanced past any appreciable damage.
(Bergman). WYOMING - Small infestation found in yard at Gillette, Campbell
County. (Fullerton). UTAH - Light in Snowville-Sage Valley area, Box Elder
County, where an outbreak occurred during 1960. Comprises 80 percent of cut-
worms infesting alfalfa in foothill areas about Providence and Millville, Cache
County. (Knowlton). COLORADO - Averaged 0-2 per square foot in alfalfa in Adams,
Larimer and Weld Counties; 0-5 per square foot in Rio Grande County. Controls
applied to few fields in Weld County. (Urano, Titensor, Gress, Jenkins).

ARMYWORM (Pseudaletia unipuncta) - MISSOURI - Counts in wheat and barley in
southeast area ranged 0-5 per square foot; larvae in first and second instars.
Egg deposition and hatching not complete. (Munson, Thomas, Wood).

WIREWORMS - UTAH - Damaging dryland wheat in Promontory area, Box Elder County.
(Knowlton). WYOMING - Causing some damage to winter and spring wheat in Campbell
County. (Lynch). NEBRASKA - Larval counts averaged 2 per square foot in alfalfa
in Gage County. (Bergman). KANSAS - Few larvae observed in fields of wheat in
Pottawatomie County. (Jones).

GRASSHOPPERS - UTAH - Few adults of Trimerotropus sp. present in farm areas of
Washington County. (Thornley). SOUTH DAKOTA - Survey on Elk Mountain range in
Custer County showed eggs to be in eye-spot to segmented stages; egg pods plenti-
ful. (Mast). WISCONSIN - Fifth-instar nymph of Chortophaga viridifasciata

collected in Rock County; this is a week earlier than similar collection in area in 1960. (Wis. Coop. Sur.). TEXAS - Nymphs of several species hatching in rather high numbers in localized areas of Falls, Bell and McLennan Counties. (Criswell).

ALFALFA WEEVIL (Hypera postica) - CONNECTICUT - Adults depositing eggs on alfalfa at Northford, New Haven County; egg hatching has begun. (Quinton, Kemmerer). PENNSYLVANIA - Averaged one adult per 10 sweeps and one larva per 40 sweeps on legumes in south central area. (Pepper). DELAWARE - Adult activity increased noticeably on untreated alfalfa throughout State; counts ranged from 3 per 10 sweeps to slightly over one per sweep. Larval feeding injury moderate to heavy in some fields in Sussex, Kent and southern New Castle Counties; ranged 2-6 larvae per stem. Feeding injury rather light in most fields in New Castle County. (Burbutis, Mason). MARYLAND - Adults and larvae gradually increasing on Eastern Shore; infestations range light to moderate. (U. Md., Ent. Dept.). WEST VIRGINIA - Damage to alfalfa ranged 10-50 percent in eastern part of State; larvae in first three instars. (W. Va. Ins. Sur.). VIRGINIA - Light to severe over Smyth County (Reynolds); medium to severe in untreated alfalfa in Wythe County (Bird); severe locally in new seeding of alfalfa in Franklin County (Welch). Larvae also locally severe in latter county. (Holdren). Larvae numbered 110 and 450, and adults 12 and 25 per 50 sweeps, in 2 fields in Washington County; larval counts in 3 fields in Russell County were 12, 250 and 3, and adults were 4, 4 and 80 per 50 sweeps. (Tarpley). SOUTH CAROLINA - Little damage reported to alfalfa in Pickens County treated during fall of 1960. Damage heavy to fields in Oconee County not treated during same period. (Nettles et al.). GEORGIA - Moderate on alfalfa in Greene County. (Shurling, Apr. 21). NEVADA - Adults continue active in Elko and northern Eureka Counties; windy weather hampering control application. (Menke). OREGON - Adults averaged 2 per 10 sweeps in alfalfa in Malheur County April 26; larvae hatching in small numbers. (Capizzi).

CLOVER LEAF WEEVIL (Hypera punctata) - PENNSYLVANIA - Fairly abundant on legumes in south central and southwest areas, with injury noticeable. (Pepper, Udine). ILLINOIS - Average larval counts per square foot in clover and alfalfa, by district, were as follows: Northwest - 12.6; northeast - 13.5; west - 16; central - 27. (Ill. Ins. Rpt.). MISSOURI - Counts in alfalfa and clover ranged 2-7 per square foot. Larvae ranged one-third grown to mature; approximately 50 percent showed evidence of a fungus disease. (Munson, Thomas, Wood). IDAHO - Late-instar larvae common in alfalfa checked in Spalding area, Nez Perce County; averaged about one per 2 sweeps. (Hawkes).

CLOVER HEAD WEEVIL (Hypera meles) - ILLINOIS - Reported for the first time this season; averaged 0.8 per 100 sweeps of clover and alfalfa in southwest area. (Ill. Ins. Rpt.). GEORGIA - Light on crimson clover in Greene County. (Shurling, Apr. 21).

LESSER CLOVER LEAF WEEVIL (Hypera nigrirostris) - ILLINOIS - Adults averaged 3.3 per 100 sweeps in clover and alfalfa in southwest area. (Ill. Ins. Rpt.). WISCONSIN - Few specimens collected in alfalfa in southwest area. (Wis. Coop. Sur.).

CLOVER ROOT CURCULIO (Sitona hispidula) - DELAWARE - First adults of season noted on alfalfa in Kent and New Castle Counties. (Burbutis, Mason). MARYLAND - Light numbers of adults noted on alfalfa in Queen Annes County. (U. Md., Ent. Dept.). VIRGINIA - Counts in alfalfa were light in 2 fields in Washington County and 3 fields in Russell County. (Tarpley). ILLINOIS - Counts per 100 sweeps of alfalfa and clover averaged 112 in west-southwest and 25 in southwest districts. (Ill. Ins. Rpt.). WISCONSIN - Few specimens collected in alfalfa in southwest area. (Wis. Coop. Sur.). NEBRASKA - Adult feeding noted on sweetclover in southeast. (Bergman).

SWEETCLOVER WEEVIL (Sitona cylindricollis) - UTAH - Causing conspicuous injury in Wasatch County and in parts of Salt Lake, Tooele and Weber Counties. (Knowlton).

PEA APHID (Macrosiphum pisi) - OREGON - Populations low in alfalfa (1-2 per sweep) in Adrian-Ontario area, Malheur County, April 26. (Capizzi). NEVADA - Variable, scattered populations averaged 0-10 per sweep in most alfalfa in Reno-Sparks area, Washoe County. Heavy infestation reported in CEIR 11(17):334 in one field near Reno continues, with severe damage to many plants in a 20-acre area. (Arnett, Bechtel, Lauderdale). COLORADO - Ranged 2-10 per 100 sweeps in Adams, Larimer and Weld Counties. (Schweissing, Jenkins). ARIZONA - Continued heavy on alfalfa statewide. (Ariz. Coop. Sur.). NEW MEXICO - Heavy infestations seriously damaging alfalfa in Virden Valley, Hidalgo County. Remains heavy in northern Dona Ana, Chaves, Eddy and Sierra Counties. (N. M. Coop. Rpt.). TEXAS - Heavy, widespread infestations on alfalfa, vetch and clover in south central, central, north central and northwest areas. Alfalfa plants in many fields heavily wilted and covered with honeydew in north central and northwest areas. Control underway in most areas. (Hatchett, Whitaker, Newton). OKLAHOMA - Moderate to heavy infestations continued common in alfalfa in most areas of State. A fungus, Entomophthorus aphidis, noted destroying 2-3 percent of population in some east central area fields; previously noted destroying one percent of population in some south central area fields checked. Det. by E. A. Steinhouse. (Okla. Coop. Sur.). ARKANSAS - Counts ranged 75-100 per sweep on alfalfa in northwest area. (Ark. Ins. Sur.). MISSOURI - Counts in alfalfa in southeast area ranged 35-90 per sweep; 25-30 percent of aphids showed symptoms of a fungus disease. Populations light in central area alfalfa; ranged 0-15 per sweep. (Munson, Thomas, Wood). NEBRASKA - Populations building up in central, south, east and southeast districts; counts as high as 50 per sweep on legumes in southeast. (Bergman). Counts approximately 10 per sweep in Lancaster County. (Stevens). ILLINOIS - Average counts per square foot in clover and alfalfa, by districts, were as follows: Northwest - 12; west - 37; central - 38; west-southwest - 102; southwest - 92. (Ill. Ins. Rpt.). INDIANA - Populations in La Porte County ranged to 30 per 25 sweeps; no alates observed. (Matthew, Lehker).

WISCONSIN - Averaged 5-6 per 25 sweeps (mostly nymphs) in alfalfa in Rock, Iowa and Lafayette Counties; averaged 20 per 25 sweeps near margin of one field of advanced alfalfa. None noted in fields in Dane County. (Wis. Coop. Sur.). VIRGINIA - Counts per 50 sweeps in 2 fields of alfalfa in Washington County were 250 and 600, and 120, 800 and 200 in 3 fields in Russell County. (Tarpley). MARYLAND - Generally light on alfalfa in all sections. Infestations to date considerably below those of 1960. (U. Md., Ent. Dept.). DELAWARE - Counts increased over previous week; ranged 30-40 per 10 sweeps in Sussex, Kent and southern New Castle Counties and 4-5 per 10 sweeps over most of latter county. (Burbutis, Mason). PENNSYLVANIA - Averaged 2 per 10 sweeps on legumes in south central area. (Pepper). NEW JERSEY - Populations increasing on alfalfa. (Ins.-Dis. Newsl., Apr. 25).

SPOTTED ALFALFA APHID (Therioaphis maculata) - ARIZONA - Infestations very low statewide. (Ariz. Coop. Sur.). NEW MEXICO - General buildup throughout southern counties. Large percent winged in Virden Valley fields, Hidalgo County. (N. M. Coop. Rpt.).TEXAS - Light and widespread on alfalfa in Yoakum County (Whitaker); light locally on alfalfa in Brazos County (Newton). OKLAHOMA - Continued moderate to heavy on alfalfa in southwest area; light to occasionally moderate in northwest, central, south central and southeast areas. No particular change noted from previous week's report. (Okla. Coop. Sur.).

SWEETCLOVER APHID (Therioaphis riehmi) - NEBRASKA - Averaged 6 per sweep in clover in Nehama and Richardson Counties. (Bergman).

YELLOW CLOVER APHID (Therioaphis trifolii) - NEBRASKA - Nymphs present in moderate numbers in red clover in east and southeast districts. (Bergman).

TARNISHED PLANT BUG (Lygus lineolaris) - ARKANSAS - Averaged 6-8 per 10 sweeps of alfalfa in northwest area; few nymphs present. Counts in vetch down from previous weeks. (Ark. Ins. Sur.). OKLAHOMA - Nymphs and adults ranged 0.5-5 per sweep in alfalfa surveyed in southeast and south central areas. (Okla. Coop. Sur.).

NEBRASKA - Adults averaged 5-20 per 10 sweeps in legumes in central, south, east and southeast districts. (Bergman). WISCONSIN - Averaged 2 per 25 sweeps in alfalfa and 2 per 50 sweeps in grain throughout most of southwest area. (Wis. Coop. Sur.). ILLINOIS - In alfalfa and clover, adults averaged 66 per 100 stems in west-southwest, 38 in southwest areas. (Ill. Ins. Rpt.). INDIANA - Adults active in alfalfa in northern areas; counts less than 5 per 25 sweeps. (Matthew, Lehker). PENNSYLVANIA - Abundant on legumes in south central area (Pepper) and in southwest area (Udine). VIRGINIA - Counts per 50 sweeps in 2 fields of alfalfa in Washington County were 20 and 20, and in 3 fields in Russell County were 31, 18 and 12. (Tarpley).

LYGUS BUGS (Lygus spp.) - UTAH - Numerous on mustards and becoming common in fields of alfalfa in Cache County; 75 percent are L. elisus. (Knowlton). NEW MEXICO - Averaged 1-2 per sweep in alfalfa in northern Dona Ana County and 5-13 per sweep in fields near Deming, Luna County. Ratio of adults to nymphs was 3 to 1. (N. M. Coop. Rpt.). TEXAS - Light, widespread infestations attacking alfalfa, oats and native pasture in Yoakum County. (Texas Coop. Rpt., Whitaker).

ALFALFA PLANT BUG (Adelphocoris lineolatus) - ILLINOIS - First observed this season in Alexander County; nymphs ranged 0-10 per 100 sweeps in clover and alfalfa. (Ill. Ins. Rpt.).

MEADOW SPITTLEBUG (Philaenus leucophthalmus) - PENNSYLVANIA - Hatching on legumes in protected locations in south central area (Pepper); some hatching in southwest (Udine). DELAWARE - First nymphs of season collected in alfalfa in New Castle County. (Burbutis, Mason). VIRGINIA - Few present in 2 fields in Washington County and in 3 fields in Russell County. (Tarpley). WEST VIRGINIA - Hatching in forage crops general over State. (W. Va. Ins. Sur.). INDIANA - Nymphs appearing in extreme northern areas. Early instar nymphs noted in La Porte, St. Joseph, Elkhart, Fulton, White, Pulaski and Starke Counties. Clover and alfalfa growth averaged 4-6 inches in height. (Lehker, Matthew). ILLINOIS - Nymphs averaged 367 per 100 sweeps of grass in southwest district. Average nymphal counts per 100 stems in clover and alfalfa, by district, were as follows: North-west - 17; northeast - 13; west - 6; central - 15; east-southeast - 2. (Ill. Ins. Rpt.).

ALFALFA CATERPILLAR (Colias eurytheme) - DELAWARE - First larvae of season noted in New Castle County. (Burbutis, Mason). NEBRASKA - Adult activity very notice-able in alfalfa and clover in east and southeast districts. (Bergman).

FORAGE LOOPER (Caenurgina erechtea) - NEBRASKA - Adults active in legumes in east and southeast districts. (Bergman). ILLINOIS - Larvae averaged 1.8 per 100 sweeps in southwest and 40 per 100 sweeps in one field in west-southwest; both counts in clover and alfalfa. (Ill. Ins. Rpt.).

GREEN CLOVERWORM (Plathypena scabra) - OKLAHOMA - Larvae ranged 0.25-2 per sweep in alfalfa surveyed in southeast and south central areas. (Okla. Coop. Sur.).

THRIPS - NEW MEXICO - Populations very high in alfalfa in Luna County; lighter in Socorro, Dona Ana, Sierra, Hidalgo and Grant Counties. (N. M. Coop. Rpt.). ILLINOIS - Averaged 17 per 100 sweeps in wheat in southwest district. (Ill. Ins. Rpt.).

TWO-SPOTTED SPIDER MITE (Tetranychus telarius) - CALIFORNIA - Medium to heavy on alfalfa generally over Imperial County. (V. Roth).

SOYBEAN CYST NEMATODE (Heterodera glycines) - VIRGINIA - Collections of 3,833 soil samples were made from a total of 2,862 acres on 98 properties. Positive collections were recorded from 12 properties, representing 900 acres in Nansemond County. (PPC, East. Reg., March Rpt.).

WHITE-FRINGED BEETLES (Graphognathus spp.) - A new infestation was found in Bolivar County, MISSISSIPPI, during March and is now being delimited. The last known infested acreage in ARKANSAS was treated during February. Minor extensions of the infested area were found in 3 counties in MISSISSIPPI and 4 counties in NORTH CAROLINA during March. (PPC, So. Reg.).

STINK BUGS - NEW MEXICO - Chlorochroa sayi, C. ligata and 2 undetermined species averaged 10-15 per plant on wild mustard near Las Cruces, Dona Ana County. (N. M. Coop. Rpt.).

FRUIT INSECTS

RED-BANDED LEAF ROLLER (Argyrotaenia velutinana) - INDIANA - Adults remained active at Terre Haute, April 20; no egg hatch to April 25. Egg hatch expected to coincide with petal fall. (Hamilton). Egg laying continues in Carbondale area; some hatching occurring. (Meyer, Apr. 26). Egg masses noted on apple trees in Tippecanoe and La Porte Counties; egg laying continues. (Matthew). WEST VIRGINIA - Emergence is slow on apple in eastern portion of State. (W. Va. Ins. Sur.). PENNSYLVANIA - Eggs less abundant on apple in south central area than during 1960; no hatching observed. (Pepper). MARYLAND - Adults and egg masses common in several commercial apple orchards in Hancock area, Washington County. (U. Md., Ent. Dept.).

PEACH TWIG BORER (Anarsia lineatella) - UTAH - Damage unusually severe on peaches in area from Santa Clara to Toquerville, Washington County, except for a few early treated orchards. (Thornley, Knowlton). Active in Ogden area, Weber County. (Davis).

ORIENTAL FRUIT MOTH (Grapholitha molesta) - CALIFORNIA - Trap collections indicate light populations occurring in Modesto area, Stanislaus County. (Cal. Coop. Rpt.).

CODLING MOTH (Carpocapsa pomonella) - INDIANA - Pupation of overwintering larvae began April 24 at Vincennes. (Hamilton).

TENT CATERPILLARS (Malacosoma spp.) - NEW YORK - Hatching in orchards in Westchester County; also hatching in numbers in Ulster County, April 21. (N. Y. Wkly. Rpt.). MARYLAND - Tents of M. americanum noticeable in untreated apple and peach orchards in Hancock area, Washington County. (U. Md., Ent. Dept.). UTAH - M. fragile damaging some untreated orchards in the "Dixie" area of Washington County. (Thornley).

PLUM CURCULIO (Conotrachelus nenuphar) - INDIANA - First adult jarred from peach tree April 24 at Vincennes. (Hamilton). Increased in Carbondale area during past few days of warm weather. (Chandler, Meyer, Apr. 26). GEORGIA - Half-grown larvae present in peaches at Reynolds, April 25; emergence of matured larvae from peach drops to enter soil to pupate should begin first week of May. There-fore, first-generation adults expected to begin emergence from soil in early June to deposit second-generation eggs latter part of that month. (Snapp).

APHIDS - MASSACHUSETTS - Several species now present on fruit buds. (Crop Pest Cont. Mess.) NEW YORK - Various species hatching in Westchester County. Anuraphis rosea observed in Orange and Ulster Counties on April 21; first observed in Niagara County, April 24; few present in apple orchards in Columbia County and hatching April 28 in Clinton County. (N. Y. Wkly. Rpt.). PENNSYLVANIA - Several species present in some untreated apple orchards in south central area. Populations decreased greatly during previous week, probably due to predators. (Pepper). WEST VIRGINIA - Eggs of various species fewer than normal on apple in eastern area; early hatched forms killed by cold weather. (W. Va. Ins. Sur.).

TARNISHED PLANT BUG (Lygus lineolaris) - INDIANA - Active on peaches at Mitchell, Lawrence County, due to ideal weather. (Marshall, Apr. 25). NEW YORK - In orchards in Orange County, April 23. (N. Y. Wkly. Rpt.).

PEAR PSYLLA (Psylla pyricola) - NEW YORK - Egg laying heavy April 23 in Orange County; eggs readily found but not abundant in Niagara County. Egg deposition relatively high in Orleans County. Egg laying has been occurring on warm days since February in Oswego County. (N. Y. Wkly. Rpt.).

FORBES SCALE (Aspidiotus forbesi) - MISSOURI - Extremely heavy in a poorly treated orchard in northeast area; several apple trees killed. (Enns).

EUROPEAN RED MITE (Panonychus ulmi) - INDIANA - Overwintering eggs hatching in Vincennes area. (Hamilton, Apr. 25). Hatching began April 24 in Carbondale area; present on oldest leaves. (Meyer, Apr. 26). WEST VIRGINIA - Number of eggs on apples in eastern area reduced by winter injury; many eggs not viable. (W. Va. Ins. Sur.). MARYLAND - Heavy on apple in an orchard at Hancock, Washington County, which did not receive delayed dormant treatment. Eggs abundant on plum at a Baltimore County location. (U. Md., Ent. Dept.). DELAWARE - Overwintering eggs hatching on apples in Sussex County. (Kelsey). PENNSYLVANIA - Very few eggs hatching on apple in south central area. (Pepper). NEW YORK - Eggs plentiful in many pear, apple, peach and sour cherry orchards in Orleans County. Populations spotty in Wayne County, with some orchards having relatively high numbers of overwintering eggs. (N. Y. Wkly. Rpt., Apr. 24).

TWO-SPOTTED SPIDER MITE (Tetranychus telarius) - INDIANA - Overwintering adults had emerged from hibernation on April 21 in Vincennes area and were feeding; eggs being laid on cover crops. (Hamilton). This and other species have emerged from hibernation in the Carbondale area. Mites now present on leaves in one orchard where overwintering numbers were high; some have migrated throughout the leafy canopy. (Meyer, Apr. 26).

CASEBEARERS - SOUTH CAROLINA - An unspecified species appears general in Orangeburg County; some tip damage present. Infestation sufficiently serious to justify controls. Numbers present indicate first brood may be very heavy. (Ferree). GEORGIA - Several species light to heavy on pecans in Lowndes, Colquitt, Dougherty, Tift and Irwin Counties. (Johnson, Apr. 18). NEW MEXICO - Overwintering generation of Acrobasis caryae infesting new shoots of pecan trees at Carlsbad, Eddy County. (N. M. Coop. Rpt.).

WALNUT HUSK FLY (Rhagoletis completa) - UTAH - Verification of identification of specimens collected from husks of black walnut at Logan, Cache County, during 1960 constitutes a new county record for this species. Presence in Tooele County during 1960 also a new county record. (Knowlton).

A MAY BEETLE (Phyllophaga sp.) - GEORGIA - Caused heavy defoliation of pecan and hickory trees in De Kalb County. (Daniels).

MEXICAN FRUIT FLY (Anastrepha ludens) - First larval infestations of season in TEXAS were found March 21 on 2 properties in Hidalgo County, 3 days earlier than during 1960. Only 2 infested grapefruit were found on each property. Larval · infestation found in grapefruit in Starr County March 28, the first infestation in the county. Infestation consisted of 8 fruits from 3 trees. First adult catches of the season were recorded during March in Brooks, Jim Wells, Webb and Willacy Counties. During March, 1,399 traps were operated on 81 properties in 11 counties. A total of 5,072 trap inspections, plus 121 grove inspections, were made during the month. A total of 110 adults (49 males and 61 females, 42 were gravid) was trapped as follows, by county: Brooks - 3; Cameron - 7; Hidalgo - 53; Jim Wells - 1; Starr - 43; Webb - 1; Willacy - 2. (PPC, So. Reg.)

In ARIZONA, trapping in the Yuma Valley and on the Yuma Mesa was negative during March. Trapping activities continued in San Diego and Imperial Counties, CALIFORNIA, during the month, with negative results. Larval inspections made on 9 properties in San Diego County were also negative. (PPC, West. Reg.). MEXICO - Trapping continued in the areas of Tijuana, Ensenada, Tecate and Mexicali, Baja California; 7,686 inspections were made of 1,875 traps on 904 properties, with negative results. Approximately 2,843 pieces of fruit were inspected at the Benjamin Hill road station in Sonora. One specimen was collected from a mammee fruit. In the Hermosillo area, Sonora, 507 fallen oranges were inspected on 4 properties, with one specimen being submitted for identification. This specimen was taken in a grove previously known to have been infested. (PPC, Mex. Reg.; March Rpt.).

CITRUS WHITEFLY (Dialeurodes citri) - MEXICO - A total of 101,896 citrus trees on 5,078 properties were inspected in the chemical and free zones of the states of Tamaulipas, Nuevo Leon, Sonora and Baja California, with 110 infested trees found on 10 properties. The second insecticide treatment was applied to 1,883 trees on 35 properties in Municipio Allende, Nuevo Leon. In the biological control zone of Municipios Guemez and Hidalgo in the State of Tamaulipas, 62,813 citrus trees were inspected on 31 properties. Infestation was found on 5,326 trees and apparently under good control by parasites. (PPC, Mex. Reg., March Rpt.).

TRUCK CROP INSECTS

BEET LEAFHOPPER (Circulifer tenellus) - WASHINGTON - Survey of overwintering populations showed host plant distribution and development to be about the same or increased over that of 1960, but beet leafhopper population was only about 20 percent of that of 1960. In some localities, tumblemustard averaged one plant per square foot and was in excellent condition for leafhopper development. The species in such areas averaged 0.9 per square foot. Populations were highest on Horse Heaven, Status, Sunnyside and Royal Slope irrigation projects. Populations were apparently low on Roza and northern Columbia Basin projects. (Klostermeyer).

SEED-CORN BEETLE (Agonoderus lecontei) - COLORADO - High population fed on sugar beet seed recently planted; approximately 100 acres required replanting in Prowers County. (Jenkin, Apr. 21).

CABBAGE LOOPER (Trichoplusia ni) - FLORIDA - Heavier on cabbage in St. Johns County than for past 3 years, but has been low on potatoes. (Workman). Apparently decreasing on untreated crucifers in Ft. Pierce area, St. Lucie County. (Hayslip).

CUTWORMS - FLORIDA - Several species have been moderate on cabbage, potato and onion in St. Johns County. This is above normal abundance. (Workman).

IMPORTED CABBAGEWORM (Pieris rapae) - GEORGIA - Heavy on broccoli locally in Spalding County. (Dupree, Apr. 19). NEW JERSEY - Adults plentiful. (Ins.-Dis. Newsl., Apr. 25).

CABBAGE SEEDPOD WEEVIL (Ceutorhynchus assimilis) - IDAHO - Adults active in Clearwater River area in west central part of State; migrating into fields in area. (Barr).

CABBAGE APHID (Brevicoryne brassicae) - GEORGIA - Moderate on cabbage in Colquitt County. (Johnson, Apr. 19). FLORIDA - Heavier this year than during past 3 years in St. Johns County. (Workman).

SOUTHERN POTATO WIREWORM (Conoderus falli) - FLORIDA - Adults appearing in numbers in light traps at Hastings, St. Johns County; were present earlier, but in low numbers. (Workman).

SOUTHERN ARMYWORM (Prodenia eridania) - FLORIDA - Infesting tomatoes on untreated plots in Ft. Pierce area, St. Lucie County; many in late instar. Commercial fields apparently free of this pest. (Hayslip).

A SERPENTINE LEAF MINER - FLORIDA - Populations low in most areas. Heavier on some treated plots at Belle Glade, Palm Beach County, than on treated plots, possibly due to insecticidal kill of parasites (Genung); population fluctuates from field to field on tomatoes at Ft. Pierce, St. Lucie County (Hayslip); appears to be increasing in Bradenton area, Manatee County, where mines are more noticeable on top portions of bean and tomato plants (Kelsheimer).

GREEN PEACH APHID (Myzus persicae) - FLORIDA - Although heavy on potatoes earlier in St. Johns County, is no longer a problem. (Workman). OKLAHOMA - Light infestations noted on some tomato and pepper plants in sale yards in northeast area. (Okla. Coop. Sur.).

MEXICAN BEAN BEETLE (Epilachna varivestis) - GEORGIA - Moderate on beans in Colquitt, Tift, Irwin and Ben Hill Counties. (Johnson, Apr. 19).

PEA APHID (Macrosiphum pisi) - DELAWARE - Present on peas in eastern Sussex County. (Burbutis, Mason).

SQUASH BUG (Anasa tristis) - TEXAS - Moderate to heavy infestations attacking young watermelon plants in Wilson County. Controls applied. (Spaniel).

BANDED CUCUMBER BEETLE (Diabrotica balteata) - FLORIDA - Becoming abundant in Homestead area, Dade County. (Wolfenbarger).

ASPARAGUS BEETLES (Crioceris spp.) - NEW JERSEY - Becoming abundant on asparagus. (Ins.-Dis. Newsl., Apr. 25). DELAWARE - First C. asparagi and C. duodecimpunctata adults of season noted on asparagus in New Castle and Sussex Counties, causing some injury to new spears. Eggs of C. asparagi also present. (Burbutis, Mason).

ONION MAGGOT (Hylemya antiqua) - NEW JERSEY - Active in southern portion of State. (Ins.-Dis. Newsl., Apr. 25).

GOLDEN NEMATODE (Heterodera rostochiensis) - NEW YORK - As the result of confirmation survey conducted during March on Long Island, 10 fields, representing 881 acres, were declared infested. (PPC, East. Reg.).

SWEETPOTATO WEEVIL (Cylas formicarius elegantulus) - ALABAMA - One new infestation was found in Covington County during March; inspections were negative in Monroe and Butler Counties. (PPC, So. Reg.).

SWEETPOTATO FLEA BEETLE (Chaetocnema confinis) - GEORGIA - Moderate on recently set sweetpotato plants in the field in Lee County. (Dupree).

A THRIPS (Frankliniella occidentalis) - CALIFORNIA - Adults medium on strawberry blooms in Encinitas, San Diego County; also heavy on onion plantings in Corona, Riverside County. (Cal. Coop. Rpt.).

SPITTLEBUGS - NEW JERSEY - Unspecified species more numerous on strawberries than during past 4 years. Populations have increased from 0.4 per 50 leaves to 11 per 50 leaves. However, numbers in most fields not sufficient to cause concern. (Ins.-Dis. Newsl., Apr. 25). DELAWARE - Philaenus leucophthalmus nymphs infesting strawberries in New Castle County. (Burbutis, Mason).

TOBACCO INSECTS

WIREWORMS - SOUTH CAROLINA - There is an apparent increasing problem on tobacco in Williamsburg County. (Nettles et al.). FLORIDA - Conoderus lividus troublesome on approximately 500 acres of tobacco at Quincy, Gadsden County; an estimated 2-3 percent loss will result. (Tappan).

TOBACCO FLEA BEETLE (Epitrix hirtipennis) - GEORGIA - Light to heavy on tobacco in the field in Berrien, Colquitt, Cook, Tift, Irwin, Ben Hill and Laurens Counties. (Johnson, Apr. 20). MARYLAND - Adults appearing in tobacco beds in Anne Arundel and St. Marys Counties. (U. Md., Ent. Dept.).

TOBACCO BUDWORM (Heliothis virescens) - GEORGIA - Light on tobacco in Berrien, Colquitt, Cook, Tift, Irwin, Ben Hill and Laurens Counties. (Johnson, Apr. 20).

CABBAGE LOOPER (Trichoplusia ni) - FLORIDA - Active on tobacco at Quincy, Gadsden County, but not serious. (Tappan).

CUTWORMS - FLORIDA - Several species more severe on shade tobacco than during 1960 at Quincy, Gadsden County. (Tappan).

HORNWORMS (Protoparce spp.) - FLORIDA - First eggs of season noted at Quincy, Gadsden County. (Tappan).

COTTON INSECTS

BOLL WEEVIL (Anthonomus grandis) - TEXAS - Cool weather early in April and dry weather during the month has not been conducive for weevil activity. One found April 24 on cotton, 3 collected from flight screens in Waco area. (Parencia et al.). Cotton is beginning to square in the lower Rio Grande Valley and adult weevils are found in most fields. (Deer).

PINK BOLLWORM (Pectinophora gossypiella) - ARIZONA The first moth of the season, a female, was taken March 20 in a light trap north of Hyder in eastern Yuma county. (PPC, West. Reg.). On April 25, three moths emerged from bolls left on ground surface in test cages at Safford, Graham County. (Ariz. Coop. Sur.).

A CUTWORM - ARIZONA - Light infestations are damaging the stands in some Pinal County fields which are following grain crops. The larvae are not in definite areas but generally scattered throughout the fields. (Ariz. Coop. Sur.).

APHIDS - TEXAS - Aphis gossypii light in 21 fields and medium in 4 fields in the Waco area. (Parencia). Light infestations of several species found in many fields in south central and south. (Deer).

COTTON FLEAHOPPER (Psallus seriatus) - TEXAS - One adult found in each of 2 fields of the 25 inspected. Sweeping records of horsemint indicate a buildup of populations on that host in the Waco area. (Parencia). Light infestation found in Jim Wells, Live Oak, San Patricio and Refugio Counties. (Deer).

THRIPS - TEXAS - Infestations of undetermined species light in 4 fields, none in 21 fields in the Waco area. (Parencia). ARIZONA - Infestations of Frankliniella occidentalis are much lighter than normal at this time on lower elevation cotton. Seedling growth is very slow because of the cool nights, but thrips migration from other hosts is very light. (Ariz. Coop. Sur.).

FOREST, ORNAMENTAL AND SHADE TREE INSECTS

EUROPEAN PINE SHOOT MOTH (Rhyacionia buoliana) - INDIANA - Larvae have moved into new bud growth in pine Christmas tree plantations in La Porte County. (Matthew).

WHITE-PINE WEEVIL (Pissodes strobi) - PENNSYLVANIA - Active in Tioga County; no egg laying observed. (Gesell).

EASTERN TENT CATERPILLAR (Malacosoma americanum) - NEW YORK - Hatched April 21-22 at Poughkeepsie on choke cherry. (N.Y. Wkly. Rpt.) PENNSYLVANIA - Beginning to form tents on cherry in the south central and southwest areas. (Udine). DELAWARE - Tents becoming quite noticeable on wild hosts throughout State. (Burbutis, Mason). VIRGINIA - Tents conspicious in crotches of wild cherry in Pittsylvania County. (Dominick). WEST VIRGINIA - Nests appearing on wild cherry throughout State. (W. Va. Ins. Sur.). ARKANSAS - Continues very active; more widespread than for many years. (Ark. Ins. Sur.). OKLAHOMA - Larvae common on wild plum in northeast area. (Okla. Coop. Sur.). ILLINOIS - Nests present throughout southern one-third of State. (Ill. Ins. Rpt.). WISCONSIN - Young larvae feeding on unopened buds of chokecherry in Iowa and Rock Counties. (Wis. Coop. Sur.).

GREAT BASIN TENT CATERPILLAR (Malacosoma fragile) - UTAH - Attacking all cotton-wood and poplar trees in warmer areas of Washington County; some trees being, nearly defoliated. (Thornley, Knowlton).

LARCH CASEBEARER (Coleophora laricella) - WISCONSIN - Observed feeding on April 23 in Dane County and as far north as Winnebago County. (Wis. Coop. Sur.).

GYPSY MOTH (Porthetria dispar) - CONNECTICUT - Eggs beginning to hatch in South Windsor area, Hartford County. (Phillips, Apr. 24).

A PHYCITID (Euzophera ostricolorella) - INDIANA - New State record; larvae boring in root collars of tulip-poplar timber trees. Complete infestation of trees over 100 acres in 2 tracts located in La Porte County. (Giese).

ELM LEAF BEETLE (Galerucella xanthomelaena) - OKLAHOMA - Overwintering adults causing some concern in homes in Deer Creek area; attacking elms in Elk City area, no egg laying noted; eggs beginning to hatch in Stillwater-Perry area; adults damaging foliage in Comanche, Murray and Kingfisher Counties. (Okla. Coop. Sur.). ARKANSAS - Appearing in small numbers in Fayetteville area. (Ark. Ins. Sur.).

COLUMBIAN TIMBER BEETLE (Corthylus columbianus) - INDIANA - Additional distribut-ion for the State: red maple in Orange, Rush and Ripley Counties; silver maple in Washington, Perry and Jackson Counties. (Giese).

ELM CALLIGRAPHA (Calligrapha scalaris) - KANSAS - Adult counts on elm sprouts in Riley County ranged 1-3 per 5-foot sprout. (Greene). OKLAHOMA - Adults attacking elms in Ponca City, Enid, Watonga and Thomas. (Okla. Coop. Sur.).

MAY BEETLES (Phyllophaga spp.) - OKLAHOMA - Adults damaging foliage on oaks and pecans in southeast area; coming to lights in northeast and north central areas. (Okla. Coop.Sur.). TEXAS - Heavy flights of adults coming to lights in Washington and Brazos Counties. Medium to heavy infestations of larvae attacking lawns in Washington County. (Texas Coop. Rpt., McClung, Newton).

A CHRYSOMELID (Chrysomela interrupta) - KANSAS - Adults very numerous on willow trees in Riley County. (Greene).

A LEAF CURL ASH APHID (Prociphilus fraxinifolii) - CALIFORNIA - Causing heavy leaf distortion on Modesto ash (Fraximus velutina glabra) in Garden Grove, Orange County. (Cal. Coop. Rpt., April 14, 1961).

AN ASH PLANT BUG (Neoborus illitus) - CALIFORNIA - Occurring as a heavy infestation of adults on ash trees in Chico, Butte County. (Cal. Coop. Rpt.).

A COSMOPTERYGID (Periploca sp.) - CALIFORNIA - An undescribed species light on Juniperus tamariscifolia in a nursery in West Covina, Los Angeles County, and in San Diego, San Diego County. These are first records south of San Joaquin County. Medium to heavy populations occurred in Vallejo, Solano County. (Cal. Coop. Rpt.).

PAINTED BEAUTY (Vanessa virginiensis) - MISSOURI - Larvae reported damaging peonies in Jasper County. (Munson, Thomas, Wood).

APHIDS - CALIFORNIA - Pemphigus bursarius medium on poplar in El Centro, Brawley and Niland, Imperial County. This is a new location for this pest of lettuce. (Cal. Coop. Rpt.).

NEW MEXICO - Macrosiphum rosae heavy on roses in Silver City area, Grant County. (N. M. Coop. Rpt.). NEVADA - Prociphilus sp. light on Modesto ash in Reno, Washoe County. Periphyllus negundinis numbers increasing on boxwood at same location. (Bechtel). OKLAHOMA - Several species continue common on a wide variety of shrubs and ornamentals in most areas. (Okla. Coop. Sur.). NORTH CAROLINA - Populations of undetermined species high on spirea, hibiscus and rose. (Bartley).

A MEMBRACID (Umbonia crassicornis) - TEXAS - Heavy local infestations on "guamuchil" (a tropical plant) in Cameron County. (Texas Coop. Rpt., Day).

COCCIDS - MARYLAND - Coccus hesperidum infesting camellias in a greenhouse at Gaithersburg, Montgomery County. (U. Md., Ent. Dept.). NORTH CAROLINA - Aspidiotus perniciosus severely infesting a 100-year-old quince in Wake County. (Clayton, Robertson). MISSOURI - A. perniciosus extremely heavy, encrusting branches of pyracantha and plum on campus at University of Missouri. Some shrubs will probably be lost. (Enns). CALIFORNIA - Pseudococcus microcirculus infesting orchids at 6 locations in Los Angeles County. Diaspis cocois heavy on Cocos plumosa in a nursery in Santa Barbara, Santa Barbara County. Aonidiella citrina heavy on ivy and light on citrus in Orlando, Glenn County. (Cal. Coop. Rpt.).

BOXWOOD LEAF MINER (Monarthropalpus buxi) - VIRGINIA - Late instars attacking boxwood in Wytheville and vicinity. Heaviest infestation noticed in years. (Bird). MARYLAND - Infesting American boxwood at Baltimore. (U. Md., Ent. Dept).

HOLLY LEAF MINERS (Phytomyza spp.) - MARYLAND - Several heavy infestations noted on various species of holly in central sections. (U. Md., Ent. Dept.).

ROSE-SLUG (Endelomyia aethiops) - OREGON - Adults were emerging and laying eggs in Salem April 24. (Goeden).

ERIOPHYID MITES - CALIFORNIA - Aceria paradianthi heavy on carnations in a nursery in Santa Barbara, Santa Barbara County. Eriophyes convolvens adults medium on Euonymus radicans in a nursery in Santa Barbara, Santa Barbara County. (Cal. Coop. Rpt.).

A SPIDER MITE (Oligonychus subnudus) - CALIFORNIA - Occurring as a medium infestation on Pinus radiata in a nursery in Colma, San Mateo County. (Cal. Coop. Rpt.).

INSECTS AFFECTING MAN AND ANIMALS

FACE FLY (Musca autumnalis) - NEW YORK - Noted April 23 and 24 on animals, man and outside of buildings; ranged 0-19 per head on cattle in barnyards. (N. Y. Wkly. Rpt.). MARYLAND - Reported on cattle for first time this season April 21 at Agricultural Research Center, Beltsville. (Mills, Fales). VIRGINIA - Common at Warm Springs, Bath County, on white automobiles. Believed to have come out of a church when the sun became warm. (Dalton). Active for over a week in Washington, Russell and Dickenson Counties. (Tarpley, Altizer, Moore). TENNESSEE - First report of season in Johnson County. (Walker). MISSOURI - Observed on livestock for the first time this season. Flies were in masses on sunny sides of houses, mailboxes, cars and other warm objects in north central area. Masses were predominately males; females probably already dispersed. (Benson). ILLINOIS - Present in several areas; counts low. (Ill. Ins. Rpt.).

HORN FLY (Haematobia irritans) - TEXAS - Counts ranged light to heavy on unsprayed cattle throughout State. (Texas Coop. Rpt.). OKLAHOMA - Averaged 100-125 per animal on 71 cows checked Pushmataha County. (Okla. Coop. Sur.). ARKANSAS - Appearing in usual numbers (Ark. Ins. Sur.). ILLINOIS - Observed in southern area; ranged 0-45 per animal. (Ill. Ins. Rpt.).

HORSE FLIES (Tabanus spp.) - OKLAHOMA - Ranged 2-4 per animal on 71 cows checked in Pushmataha County. (Okla. Coop. Sur.).

STABLE FLY (Stomoxys calcitrans) - ARKANSAS - Appearing in usual numbers. (Ark. Ins. Sur.).

CATTLE GRUBS (Hypoderma spp.) - NEW MEXICO - Adults of H. lineatum more numerous this spring than for several years in Grant County. (N. M. Coop. Rpt.). TEXAS - H. lineatum adults continue to annoy cattle throughout State. (Texas Coop. Rpt.). OKLAHOMA - Adults of H. lineatum continue to annoy cattle throughout State. (Okla. Coop. Sur.). UTAH - Control for these pests in Cache County applied to 11,000 dairy animals and 12,000 beef animals. (Knowlton).

SCREW-WORM (Callitroga hominivorax) - TEXAS - Generally widespread over south and south central areas. (Texas Coop. Rpt.). NEW MEXICO - Reports from several ranchers in Grant County indicate problems on newborn calves, animals following branding and animals with wounds. (N. M. Coop. Rpt.).

MOSQUITOES - MISSOURI - Very heavy populations of Aedes spp. observed in southeast area. (Munson, Thomas, Wood).

AN ASSASSIN BUG (Melanolestes picipes) - OKLAHOMA - Adults causing annoyance around some homes in the Stillwater area. (Okla. Coop. Sur.).

TICKS - UTAH - Dermacentor andersoni annoying humans in Washington and Tooele Counties. (Thornley, Knowlton). SOUTH DAKOTA - D. variabilis a problem on dogs in Aurora area, Brookings County. (Walstrom). NEBRASKA - D. variabilis occurring on children and dogs in residential areas of Lincoln, Lancaster County. (Bergman). OKLAHOMA - Counts of Amblyomma americanum ranged 20-30 per animal on 71 cows checked in Pushmataha County. (Okla. Coop. Sur.).

STORED-PRODUCT INSECTS

INDIAN-MEAL MOTH (Plodia interpunctella) - ARIZONA - Heavy infestation reported in a Phoenix feed mill. (Ariz. Coop. Sur.). OKLAHOMA - Infesting a variety of cereal products in some homes in Stillwater area. (Okla. Coop. Sur.).

MEDITERRANEAN FLOUR MOTH (Anagasta kuhniella) - OKLAHOMA - Infesting a variety of cereal products in some homes in the Stillwater area. (Okla. Coop. Sur.).

DERMESTIDS (Trogoderma spp.) - ARIZONA - Heavy infestations of several species other than T. granarium in some Maricopa County feed mills. (Ariz. Coop. Sur.).

LESSER GRAIN BORER (Rhyzopertha dominica) - TEXAS - Light to moderate local infestations of adults attacking stored milo in Smith County. (Texas Coop. Rpt.).

BENEFICIAL INSECTS

HYMENOPTEROUS PARASITES - ARKANSAS - Large numbers of various species present. (Ark. Ins. Sur.). OKLAHOMA - Populations of Aphidius testaceipes increasing in fields of small grain in northwest area. (Okla. Coop. Sur.). NEW MEXICO - In one field in Eddy County with a light to moderate infestation of spotted alfalfa aphid, 3-5 aphids parasitized by Praon palitans were found per square foot. (N. M. Coop. Rpt.) OREGON - Two shipments of Aphidius spp., parasites of pea aphid, were released at a site near Corvallis week of April 23. (Ritcher). WASHINGTON - Aphidius pisivorus on pea aphids in alfalfa; adults found in almost every alfalfa field but not in sufficient numbers to prevent aphid flight to peas, in Walla Walla and Gardena. (Woodworth).

LADY BEETLES - NEW YORK - Fairly active in small fruit orchards April 27. (N.Y. Wkly. Rpt.). ILLINOIS - Adults averaged 32 per 100 sweeps in clover and alfalfa in west-southwest and 6 per 100 sweeps in the southwest. Larvae were observed for the first time this year; averaged 3 per 100 sweeps in southwest. Adults averaged 3 per 100 sweeps in wheat in same area. (Ill. Ins. Rpt.). ARKANSAS - Fewer in numbers than normal. (Ark. Ins. Sur.). NEW MEXICO - Adults and larvae very abundant in barley infested with corn leaf aphid in northern Dona Ana County. Very abundant in alfalfa heavily infested with pea aphid in Virden Valley, Hidalgo County. (N. M. Coop. Rpt.). OREGON - Several species averaged one per five sweeps in Malheur County alfalfa fields April 26. (Capizzi). INDIANA - Hippodamia convergens feeding on aphids and scales. (Hamilton, April 20). VIRGINIA - Coleomegilla maculata fuscilabris and Coccinella novemnotata light in 2 fields each of alfalfa in Washington and Russell Counties. (Tarpley).

NABIDS (Nabis spp.) - ILLINOIS - Counts averaged 23 per 100 sweeps in clover and alfalfa in west-southwest, 8 in the southwest. (Ill. Ins. Rpt.). VIRGINIA - N. ferus light in Washington and Russell Counties. (Tarpley).

LACEWINGS - INDIANA - Adults active in orchards at Vincennes April 20. (Hamilton) ILLINOIS - Counts averaged 2 per 100 sweeps in clover and alfalfa in west-southwest and 5 in the southwest. (Ill. Ins. Rpt.). ARKANSAS - Chrysopa spp. adults are numerous but there is little evidence of reproduction. (Ark. Ins. Sur.).

SYRPHIDS - INDIANA - Adults active at Vincennes on April 20 in orchards. (Hamilton). ILLINOIS - Larvae observed for the first time this year. Counts averaged 2 per 100 sweeps in clover and alfalfa in southwest. (Ill. Ins. Rpt.). ARKANSAS - Adults and larvae rather common. (Ark. Ins. Sur.).

MISCELLANEOUS INSECTS

SUBTERRANEAN TERMITES (Reticulitermes spp.) - NEVADA - Infestations of Reticulitermes sp. found in ten homes in Elko, Elko County. (Menke). MISSOURI - R. flavipes reported swarming throughout State. (Munson, Thomas, Wood). NORTH CAROLINA - R. flavipes swarming in a house in Catawba County. (Farrier). IDAHO - R. hesperus infesting basement of a home at Nampa, Canyon County. (Bechtolt).

BOXELDER BUG (Leptocoris trivittatus) - WYOMING - Adults very numerous in many areas of State. (Fullerton). SOUTH DAKOTA - Numerous complaints being received. (Mast).

ALLEGHENY MOUND ANT (Formica exsectoides) - MARYLAND - Several mounds noted at Lock Raven, Baltimore County. (U. Md., Ent. Dept.).

CARPET BEETLES - NORTH DAKOTA - Numerous home infestations of unspecified species continue to be reported from many localities. (N. D. Ins. Sur.).

MAY BEETLES - TENNESSEE - Large numbers appearing across State, especially heavy in Shelby County. (Mullett).

OLD-HOUSE BORER (Hylotrupes bajulus) - PENNSYLVANIA - Reported from a home in York County. (Pepper).

CORRECTION

CEIR 11(16):318 - SPOTTED ALFALFA APHID - NEW MEXICO - This note should read: PEA APHID (Macrosiphum pisi) extremely heavy and killing seedling and established stands of alfalfa in Virden Valley, Hidalgo County. (N. M. Coop. Rpt.).

LIGHT TRAP COLLECTIONS

	Pseud. unip.	Agrot. ips.	Feltia subterr.	Perid. saucia	Prod. ornith.	Protoparce sexta	quinq.	Helic zea
ARIZONA								
Mesa 4/17-23				11	11			13
ARKANSAS								
Morrilton 4/20-26	35	14		16				5
Kelso 4/20-26	6	2		6				2
Fayetteville 4/20-26	83	60		26				2
COLORADO								
New Liberty 4/16-26	1	19						
Two Buttes 4/16-26	3	18		47				
FLORIDA								
Monticello 4/25			1		5			1
ILLINOIS (County)								
Champaign 4/21-27	59	11		1				
KANSAS								
Garden City 4/15-20, 24, 25	1	11		23				
Hays 4/20, 22, 23	3			5				
Manhattan 4/22-27	7	5		8				
Mound Valley 4/20,25	64	21		12				
Wathena 4/18-25	18			10				
MISSISSIPPI								
*Stoneville 4/21-27	645	73	6	152	33	11	1	10
NEBRASKA								
North Platte 4/13-20		32		18				
SOUTH CAROLINA								
Clemson 4/22-28	13	4	1	15	1			
Charleston 4/24-30	1	6	4		3			1
TENNESSEE (Counties)								
Monroe 4/18-24	178	1		22	9			
Maury 4/18-24	201	10		17	2			
Robertson 4/18-24	36	4		8				
Cumberland 4/18-24	20	12		7	1			
Greene 4/18-24	17	3		10				
Johnson 4/18-24	8	7		3	1			
TEXAS								
Waco 4/14-20	8	10	18	17	7			9
Waco 4/22-28	4	2	17	15	17			6
Brownsville 4/21	6	43	265	28	9	10		239
WISCONSIN								
Mazomanie 4/25	15			1				

In the interest of survey methods improvement we are publishing "Survey Methods for Survey Entomologists", a guide developed for the North Central States, originating with the Insect Survey and Losses Committee of the North Central States Branch of the Entomological Society of America. The committee membership consists of Clarence E. White, Chairman, O. H. Hammer and Leroy L. Peters. Mr. White's address is Survey Entomologist, Section of Economic Entomology, 280 Natural Resources Building, Urbana, Illinois.

The committee should be commended for its efforts to assemble a preliminary survey guide for survey and field entomologists. There will be supplemental sections. The chairman's letter of transmittal reads in part, "Our committee would certainly appreciate having any comments on the present article and would also be glad to have suggestions on methods of surveying for livestock and stored grain insects as methods of surveying for these two groups of insects are now being written."

Survey and Detection Operations believes this survey guide, though incomplete, marks a strong beginning and we are hopeful it will stimulate nationwide interest in this subject. There is a real need for a complete and usable survey guide. Separates are available upon request.

****

SURVEY METHODS FOR SURVEY ENTOMOLOGISTS

Since 1953, survey entomologists have been employed on a State-Federal cooperative basis in several states. These entomologists were given the responsibility of checking on insect populations within their respective states. This was to serve as both a warning and detection system. This was to warn the farmers when and where insect populations were reaching the damaging point in order that timely treatments could be applied. It was also to try to detect the presence of any new insect pest which might enter the state.

Many valuable contributions have been made and the system should become more valuable as it gains in expereience. However, most survey methods which have been published are concerned with making intensive surveys for one species of insect. Examples are fall grasshopper and chinch bug survey mthods. This is only natural because such specific surveys have been conducted for many years. The survey entomologists, however, were not employed to take over these specific surveys but were intended to do general survey work on all insect pests, potential pests, and new introductions.

Obviously, general surveys cannot be made by the same intensive methods used for specific surveys. If survey entomologists are to make progress they must revise their thinking and methods to fit the general type of surveys. This does not mean that the old, specific survey methods should be abandoned. These methods are unsurpassed for the specific insect survey for which they were intended. General insect surveys, however, must be looked upon as something new and progressive, and must adopt methods suitable for their purposes. It is with this view in mind that the Insect Surveys and Losses Committee of the North-Central Branch, Entomological Society of America, has written the following suggested instructions for survey entomologists, especially beginners. We realize that improvements, additions, and revisions will be necessary from time to time.

Selecting the Field or Other Survey Location

Since it is the duty of a survey entomologist to cover an entire state, some
practical method must be adopted as a guide in selecting the fields or locations
to be surveyed.

All general surveys should be made on a district basis and not on a county basis.
Therefore, the state should be divided into districts, as northwest, northeast,
central, etc. The establishment of districts can be done in several ways. They
may be the Crop Reporting Districts already established in most states or they
can be established on a climatic, ecological, geographic or some other basis.
The main point to keep in mind is that the report written by the survey entomologist is for the public benefit; therefore, the districts must be the same for
all insects in order to avoid confusion. The ideal situation would be to survey
50 to 100 locations well distributed over a district. However, this is imprac-
tical for the survey entomologist who will have to survey two or three districts
in a week's time. The only practical alternative is to take as good a cross
section of each district as possible. This will probably mean following one
highway across the district, although it may sometimes be possible to re-cross
the same district on another highway on the return trip. The first step, therefore, is to decide the districts to be surveyed during the week; second, decide
the highways to be followed; third, space fields or other survey locations about
equidistance apart along the highway. The actual number of miles apart may vary
from 10 to 15 to 25, or more, depending on the crops, etc., to be surveyed and
total distance to be traveled. Thus, if the survey is to be made only in clover
and alfalfa, the fields may be spaced closer together than if clover-alfalfa,
small grain, and corn fields and livestock are to be examined. In the latter
example a field or herd of each type would be examined.

In emergencies one crop may be given some priority over other crops in the week's
survey but should never be given such high priority as to exclude surveys in
other crops. There are already too many examples where this has been done and
invariably an outbreak occurred in the excluded crops thus catching the survey
entomologist completely off guard.

One important point which must be remembered is this: Always be on the lookout
for signs of insect damage while driving from one survey location to another.
If a suspicious situation is observed, stop and examine it immediately. In this
way it may be possible to find localized infestations which may otherwise be
missed completely. Likewise leave enough flexibility in the plans to permit
examining any infestation brought to your attention by other persons, unless
this has also shown up in the normal day's work. Do not follow the same highway
every time a district is surveyed, and do not return to the same field each time.
However, the same location may be examined more than once during the season. In
the actual selection of the survey point, survey the first easily accessible
field, bin site, herd, etc., beyond some town, highway junction, etc. In some
cases, after the general location of the survey point has been selected it will
be necessary to contact the owner before making the actual survey. For example,
if you are surveying for lice or grubs on cattle it would be necessary to have
the cattle confined. The local county agent would probably be helpful in making
arrangements with the herd owner after the general location has been selected.

The actual method for making the survey once you have arrived at the pre-selected
location will be discussed later under the specific titles of "Cereal and Forage
Crops", "Livestock Insects", etc.

Identification of Insects

If a species of insect is found in fair numbers and is suspected of causing
damage to the crop, or if any insect suspected of being a new pest in the state
is found but the species is not recognized, check with other state personnel and
the state collection. If the specimens are still not identified, send them to
the Insect Identification and Parasite Introduction Branch, A.R.S., U.S.D.A.,
Beltsville, Maryland, for identification.

How to Prepare Insects for Shipment

The following list should be followed, insofar as practicable in preparing insects for preservation and shipment.

All members of the following insect orders should be pinned or mounted on points, depending upon size, with the exceptions noted:

Coleoptera (except the following families which should be preserved in alcohol: Anobiidae, Anthicidae, Buprestidae, Chrysomelidae, Curculionidae, Dermestidae, Euglenidae, Meloidae, Nitidulidae, Ptilinidae, and Scarabaeidae. Erotylidae should be packed in pill boxes).

Diptera (all wingless parasitic flies and nematocerous adults, except Culicidae, in alcohol; Psychodidae, in pill boxes).

Orthoptera (except roaches--see below).

Hymenoptera (except ants, which should be in alcohol).

Lepidoptera (except Olethreutidae, Saturniidae, Sphingidae, and Ageriidae, which should be in envelopes; all adults less than 1 cm. wing span in pill boxes).

Hemiptera	Mecoptera
Odonata	Trichoptera

All members of the following insect orders should be preserved and shipped in alcohol, with the exceptions noted:

Homoptera (except cicadas, which should be pinned).

Orthoptera (roaches only--pin one specimen from each series).

Collembola	Dermaptera	Siphonaptera
Zoraptera	Embioptera	Ephemeroptera
Plecoptera	Mallophaga	
Isoptera	Anoplura	

Also preserved in alcohol should be larvae and pupae of all holometabolous insects, as well as all ticks and mites, and other arthropods such as centipedes, millipedes, scorpions, etc. Also place in the container a small slip of paper giving the name of the crop from which the specimens were taken, the date they were taken, the name of the town nearest to which they were taken, county and state, and whether they were up on the plants, on the surface of the soil under the plants, or in the soil around the roots of the plants. The name of the collector should also appear on the paper. A piece of paper 1 inch by 2 inches or less would be satisfactory. A sample label reads as follows: Clover field soil surface, June 5, 1958, Urbana, Champaign County, Illinois, John Doe. If a sufficient number of specimens are collected keep some in the office labeled in the same way, so when the identification is returned it can be associated with the proper insects.

These properly identified and labeled insects can then be kept in the office for future reference or as an aid in identifying this species if it is taken again at some later date.

Forms for Recording of Field Data

At the present time there are as many different forms used as there are survey entomologists. Some prefer a rather simple form which is suitable for recording any insect found on any crop. An example of a form of this type is shown on page 370. Its advantage is that only one form needs to be carried. The disadvantages are an increased amount of writing in the field, difficulty in summarizing the data, and difficulty of rechecking the data at a later date. The other extreme is a special form for each crop (page 371). Its disadvantage is the necessity of carrying several forms. Distinguishing between the various forms in the field is easily done, however, if the form for each crop is on a specific color of paper. The advantages are very little writing in the field, ease of summarizing data, and ease of filing and rechecking if needed later, and also it serves as a reminder to check on certain insects. Between these two extremes many variations are now in use. There is apparently much dissatisfaction with the forms now being used by most survey entomologists. However, the type of form used is strictly a matter of personal preference.

A yearly summary sheet has also proved useful to some survey entomologists (page 372). This form is made out for each species of insect. It can be filed easily and offers a quick and ready reference for the abundance of that species in all districts of the state covered each week.

These survey methods are not intended for use in determining the need for control in an individual field or specific location but only for determining the general situation in a given area. However, by repeating the described survey at enough different places in the field or specific location to obtain a fair cross section of the population these same methods can be used to determine need for treating individual fields, herds, bin sites, etc.

CEREAL AND FORAGE INSECTS

Surveying the Field After it is Located

Enter the field at the most accessible spot. If there is a possibility of insects migrating into the field from the roadsides, etc., take at least one sample in the margin of the field, then go at least 25 steps into the field and take 2 or 3 samples at least 25 steps apart. (Actual methods for taking samples are given below under "Sampling Methods for Insects Found in Specific Crops.") If a field is entered at or near a corner, take the marginal sample, then proceed toward the center of the field for at least 50 paces before taking the remaining samples.

In addition to recording insect populations record the height or stage of development of the plants, damage being done by the insects if possible, and any unusual weather conditions, such as very dry, wet, unusually windy, etc. Always look for new or unusual insects and while moving from one sample spot to another, visually examine the surrounding crop for signs of damage or any unusual appearance.

Sampling Methods for Insects Found in Clover, Alfalfa, Grass and Similar Low-Growing Forage Crops

1. The sweep method: This is by far the most widely used and the most popular method for most insects. It can also be used in small grain fields. A sweep consists of a half circle or 180°-swing with the hoop of a 15-inch net, held in a vertical plane with the lower half sweeping into the crop. The handle of the net should be a standard 36-inch length. The net should be held in one hand with the hand about a foot from the top of the handle. The protruding end of the handle should rest along the forearm toward the elbow. A two-handed sweep of the same size is permissible but be careful of the tendency to prescribe a smaller circle when using two hands. Until proficiency in counting insects is acquired, the insects should be counted after each sweep. Later, after much

experience in sweeping and counting, it will be possible to make one or two trial sweeps and determine whether it will be necessary to count the insects in each sweep or if more sweeps, possibly five or ten, can be taken before a count is necessary. The number of sweeps taken before a count is made depends on the abundance of insects and the surveyor's ability to count them before they escape from the net. At first it will be necessary to concentrate on counting one or two species after each sweep. With a little experience it will be possible to count several species after each sweep. Count the quick flying or jumping insects such as tarnished plant bug adults and grasshoppers first and the slow moving larval forms last.

The number of sweeps to take in each field is also determined by the abundance of the insects. Usually ten sweeps are sufficient to establish the general population for any species. However, in some cases like in establishing the early population of the potato leafhopper or spotted alfalfa aphid, it may be necessary to take anywhere frym 100 to 500 sweeps in a field. A good policy to follow is this: Make five or ten counts. Thus, if the insect is so abundant that it must be counted after each sweep, it would only be necessary to make five or ten sweeps to determine its general population. However, if the species is so scarce that you can take twenty sweeps before counting, it would be necessary to make 100 to 200 sweeps to determine the general population. Estimate extremely high populations of aphids by counting the number on a small part of the net, then based on that figure, estimate the total number in the net.

In order to keep all reports on an equal basis, regardless of how many sweeps are taken, report the number of insects per 100 sweeps. Thus, if five insects are found in ten sweeps, report it as 50 insects per 100 sweeps, or if two insects are found in 200 sweeps report it as 1 insect per 100 sweeps. The one exception is aphids, where, due to the extremely high populations sometimes found, they may be reported as aphids per sweep.

The sweep method is used for all lepidopterous larvae (except certain cutworms and webworms which feed near the soil surface), aphids, all leafhopper adults and nymphs, spittlebug adults, membracids, most beetle adults and larvae (except adults and larvae of clover leaf weevil and root feeding species), hemipterous adults and nymphs, and small grasshopper nymphs in foliage more than 5 to 6 inches in height.

2. The square foot method: This method is slower and more tedious than the sweep method but is necessary in establishing the population of some insects, especially during the late winter or early spring. It consists of measuring off a square foot on the ground and counting all the insects within the square foot area. It is suggested that a wire may be bent to form a frame measuring 1 foot on each side, and this frame then used to measure off the square foot area. A circular hoop enclosing a square foot of area may be used. One to three 1-square-foot samples in a field is sufficient for general survey work. Report the average number of insects per square foot in the field. The square foot method is used for aphids when foliage is less than 3 to 4 inches in height, cutworms (variegated can usually be counted by sweep method also), clover leaf weevil larvae and adults (although the sweep method can be used for adults), Sitona adults when plant growth is less than 3 or 4 inches and by sifting the top 3 or 4 inches of soil for larvae.

3. The stem count method: This method is necessary to establish the population of certain nymphs and larvae. It consists of counting all the insects or damage found on individual clover or alfalfa stems. A total of 10 to 100 stems should be examined. Do not examine all the stems in one spot but examine a group of 5 to 10 stems, then move to another spot and repeat. Report the number of insects per 100 stems. The stem count is used for spittlebug nymphs and lesser clover leaf weevil larvae.

4. The root count method: This is designed exclusively for the clover root borer. It consists of dissecting a total of at least 10 roots taken from two or more spots in the field. Count the number of larvae, pupae, and adults found and report on the number of each form per 100 roots.

5. The Berlese funnel is useful in determining overwintering populations of insects. Plants are carefully cut off at ground level and put in a paper sack, along with trash from the ground around the plants. Return the plant materials to the laboratory and put in the Berlese funnel, where the heat causes the insects to leave the plants and fall into the collection bottle. Report as so many insects per 100 plants. The Berlese funnel is also useful in checking overwintering populations of insects in grass sod or in trash along fence rows or in woodland areas where many forage crop insects hibernate. In these situations it is best to take a square foot of sod or a square yard of surface trash and report accordingly.

Sampling Methods for Insects Found in Corn and Sorghum Fields

1. Survey method for insects found above ground: Count all insects found on 25 (100-200 in a few cases) consecutive plants, plant whorls, ears or heads, depending on the feeding habits. Determine and report the percent of plants, etc., which are infested or damaged, and the number of insects per 100 plants, ears, etc. This method is used for corn flea beetle, Japanese beetle adults, chinch bugs, corn rootworm adults, corn earworm (100 to 200 plants if checking whorl feeding), fall armyworm (100 to 200 plants if checking whorl feeding), armyworm, grasshoppers, corn leaf aphid (estimated number per tassel, whorl, and/or leaf), thrips, European corn borer egg masses, European corn borer larvae by determining number of larvae on or in two infested plants then multiply times percent of plants infested times 100 to get borers per 100 plants, sorghum webworm, sorghum midge, and predatory insects.

2. Survey method for insects found below ground level: This survey is designed to determine insect abundance and stand damage. It is used mainly for early season work when the plants are small. Determine the percent of plants damaged by examination of 100 consecutive plants at two places (200 plants in all) 25 to 50 rows apart. In heavy infestations where possibly a fourth or a fifth of the plants are damaged, an examination of 25 plants each place should be sufficient. This examination can be made very rapidly as you walk along the row. Look for plants which are stunted, wilting, dying, cut off, etc. Determine the number of larvae per damaged plant by examining the roots, and soil about the roots, of at least two damaged plants in each group of the plants examined. Multiply the average number of larvae per damaged plant times the percent of plants infested, times 100, to get the average number of larvae per 100 plants. Report the percent of plants damaged, larvae per damaged plant, and worms per 100 plants. This method is used for cutworms, rootworms, white grubs, Japanese beetle larvae, Maecolaspis larvae, root aphids, and other root feeding insects.

Sampling Methods for Insects Found in Small Grain Fields

The principal method used in small grain insect surveys is the linear foot of drill row in drilled grain or the square foot in broadcast grain fields. However, sweeps and head counts can also be used.

1. The linear foot method: Very carefully examine 1 linear foot of row at five different places in the field and count all insects found. It will be necessary to pull the trash away from the base of the plants to find certain larvae hiding in the trash or on the ground under trash. Report the number of insects per 100 linear feet, except aphids and chinch bugs which are reported as the numer per one linear foot. The linear foot method is used for armyworms, cutworms, wireworms (by searching in soil), aphids, chinch bugs, mites, and predatory insects.

2. The square foot method: This is the same as the linear foot method except a square foot is used instead of a linear foot. Use only where grain is broadcast. Report per square foot.

3. The sweep method: Sweeps are made in the same manner as previously described for clover, alfalfa, and grass insects. The sweep method in grain can be used after grain reaches a height of four to five inches for aphids, very small armyworms and predatory insects.

4. The head count method: Count the insects on 10 to 25 heads which are selected at random. Report the number per 100 heads. This method is used for aphids, especially the English grain aphid and in grain sorghum for lepidopterous larvae and sorghum midge.

5. The leaf count: Perhaps in extremely high populations of mites, aphids, or thrips, it may be more satisfactory to determine the population by counting the number on 10 to 25 randomly selected leaves and reporting number per 100 leaves rather than trying to determine the number per linear foot.

Sampling Methods for Insects Found in Soybeans

1. The linear foot method: Carefully examine all plants on five linear feet of row at two or more places in the field and count all insects found. When the plants are large, bend them over the space between the rows and shake them vigorously, then count the insects on the ground between the rows. Insects like the bean leaf beetle will fly or hide quickly once they are shaken from the plants. Therefore, it is best to shake only a few plants at a time. Report the number of insects per 100 linear feet of row. The linear foot method is used for all leaf feeding insects especially when the plants are less than six inches high and for root feeding insects by examining roots and soil about the roots. The most important insects of which the adults may be found feeding on the leaves and the larvae feeding on the roots are bean leaf beetle, a grape colaspis, Phyllophaga, Japanese beetle and Sitona. Larvae of the green cloverworm, grasshoppers, southern corn rootworm adults, plant bugs, and stink bugs may be found feeding on blossoms, pods or leaves.

2. The sweep method: The sweep in soybeans differs from that in clover and alfalfa. In soybeans a sweep is taken along one row of beans. As the surveyor stands facing a row he reaches over the first row and sweeps the net along the second row from left to right as far as he can reach in both directions. Count the insects after each sweep as it is difficult to move from one row to another without some insects escaping from the net. Report the number of insects per 100 sweeps. This method is useful in checking populations of bean leaf beetle adults, southern corn rootworm adults, grape colaspis adults, Japanese beetle adults, leafhopper adults and nymphs, grasshoppers, green cloverworm larvae, plant bugs, stink bugs, and predatory insects.

INSECT SURVEY STOP-RECORD

SURVEYOR

Stop No.	Date	County	Location or Field No.	Crop	Insects and Population	Remarks

CLOVER AND ALFALFA INSECT SURVEY IN ILLINOIS

District _____ Date _____ Observer _____

								Total	Ave.
Temp. __ to __ °F		County							
Fair, Ptly.Cldy.,Cldy		Crop							
Pl. Height __ to __ in.		Damage							
Alf. Cat. Larvae		100SW							
		Living	Sq. Ft.						
	Pea	Living	100Sw.						
		Dead	%						
	Spotted	Living	100Le.						
*Aphids	Alfalfa	Living	100Sw.						
		Dead	%						
	Sweet Clover		100Sw.						
	Yellow Clover		Sq.Ft.						
			100Sw.						
Blister		Black	100Sw.						
Beetle		Margined	100Sw.						
Adults		Stripped	100Sw.						
	Larvae	Living	Sq.Ft.						
*Clover		Dead	Sq.Ft.						
leaf	Cocoons	Living	Sq.Ft.						
Weevil		Dead	Sq.Ft.						
	Adults	Living	Sq.Ft.						
		Living	100Sw.						
Cl. Head Cat	Adults		100Sw.						
Cl. Head Weev.	Adults		100Sw.						
Clover		Adults	100Sw.						
Root		Adults	100Rt.						
Borer		Pupae	100Rt.						
		Larvae	100Rt.						
Cutworm		Variegated	Sq.Ft.						
Larvae			100Sw.						
		Others	Sq.Ft.						
Flea Beetle Adults			100Sw.						
Forage Looper Larvae			100Sw.						
*Grape Colaspis Adults			100Sw.						
*Grasshoppers			Sq.Yd.						
			100Sw.						
Gr. Cloverworm Larvae			100Sw.						
*Hypera Nigrir.	Adults		100Sw.						
Hypera meles		Adults	100Sw.						
*H. nigr.&mel.Lar.*Stms.			Inf.						
*Meadow		Adults	100Sw.						
Spittlebug		Nymphs	100St.						
*Plant		Alfalfa	100Sw.						
Bug		Rapid	100Sw.						
Adults		Tarnished	100Sw.						
*Plant Bug Nymphs			100Sw.						
*Potato		Adults	100Sw.						
Leafhopper		Nymphs	100Sw.						
		Sweet	Sq.Ft.						
*Sitona		Clover	100Sw.						
Adults		All	Sq.Ft.						
		Others	100Sw.						
Tortricid Larvae			100Sw.						
Damsel Bugs		All Forms	100Sw.						
Lacewings		Adults	100Sw.						
		Larvae	100Sw.						
Lady		Adults	100Sw.						
Beetles		Larvae	100Sw.						
Syrphid Fly Larvae			100Sw.						

Clover Leaf Weevil Larval Populations in Clover and Alfalfa Fields of
Illinois, 1960
Average number living larvae per square foot.

Date	Section of State									Wt.ed. state Av.	Range by fields	Tot. No. flds.	Damage
	NW	NE	W	C	E	WSW	ESE	SW	SE				
Feb. 26-Mar. 3													
March 4-10													
" 11-17													
" 18-24													
" 25-31													
Apr. 1-7													
" 8-14													
" 15-21													
" 22-28													
Apr. 29-May 5													
May 6-12													
" 13-19													
" 20-26													
" 27-June 2													
June 3-9													
" 10-16													
" 17-23													
" 24-30													
July 1-7													
" 8-14													
" 15-21													
" 22-28													
" 29-Aug. 4													
Aug. 5-11													
" 12-18													
" 19-25													
" 26-Sept. 1													
Sept. 2-8													
" 9-15													
" 16-22													
" 23-29													
" 30-Oct. 6													
Oct. 7-13													
" 14-20													
" 21-27													
" 28-Nov. 3													

Notes:

UNITED STATES DEPARTMENT OF AGRICULTURE
WASHINGTON 25, D. C.

Official Business

POSTAGE AN

U. S. Dept. of Agr. Library
Beltsville Branch
7-16-58 Plant Industry Station
IPS Beltsville, Md.

CPSIA information can be obtained
at www.ICGtesting.com
Printed in the USA
BVHW091628121118
532888BV00015B/503/P

9 780428 963972